Searchlight BOOKS™

My Style

My Awesome Hair and Nails

Lakita Wilson

Lerner Publications ◆ Minneapolis

Lerner Publications Company
An imprint of Lerner Publishing Group, Inc.
241 First Avenue North
Minneapolis, MN 55401 USA

For reading levels and more information, look up this title at www.lernerbooks.com.

Main body text set in Adrianna Regular.
Typeface provided by Chank.

Library of Congress Cataloging-in-Publication Data

Names: Wilson, Lakita, author.
Title: My awesome hair and nails / Lakita Wilson.
Description: Minneapolis : Lerner Publications, [2022] | Series: Searchlight books— my style | Includes bibliographical references and index. | Audience: Ages 8–11 | Audience: Grades 2–3 | Summary: "How can we keep our hair and nails looking great and feeling healthy? Readers learn the latest tips and tricks in hairstyling and nail art, and the meaning behind current and historical styles"— Provided by publisher.
Identifiers: LCCN 2020009966 (print) | LCCN 2020009967 (ebook) | ISBN 9781728404202 (library binding) | ISBN 9781728418636 (ebook)
Subjects: LCSH: Hairdressing—History—Juvenile literature. | Hair—History—Juvenile literature. | Nails (Anatomy)—Juvenile literature.
Classification: LCC GT2295 .W55 2020 (print) | LCC GT2295 (ebook) | DDC 391.5— dc23

LC record available at https://lccn.loc.gov/2020009966
LC ebook record available at https://lccn.loc.gov/2020009967

Manufactured in the United States of America
1-48478 48992-5/17/2021

Table of Contents

Chapter 1

HAIR AND NAIL HISTORY

Since ancient times, people have used their hair and nails to show off their style. But for many, hairstyles and nail art showed more than just style. They also revealed someone's social status, job, or membership in a certain group. Around the world, hair and nail styles have evolved over time.

In ancient Egypt, many men and women shaved their heads. When they left their homes, they wore hair extensions and wigs made of human hair or sheep's wool. Women braided and decorated their wigs with gold and ivory hairpins and jewels. They used plant juices to color their wigs blue, green, and gold.

As shown in this ancient Egyptian tomb painting, Egyptians wore headpieces around their hair or wigs.

Long nails were a symbol of wealth in Egypt. Wealthy women wore nail extensions of gold, ivory, and bone. Everyone used nail colors made with henna dye and berries, but the color red was reserved for the wealthy. Like the Egyptians, women in India, Pakistan, and Middle Eastern countries decorated their fingertips with henna.

HENNA IS STILL USED FOR MANY CULTURAL REASONS, INCLUDING IN CELEBRATIONS SUCH AS WEDDINGS.

Ancient Romans used hairpieces to make their hair appear thicker or longer. Originally, Roman women used simple hairstyles. Over time, women began using jeweled hairpins to arrange their hair in elaborate styles when going out. Sometimes they wore their hair down in ringlets. They lightened their hair with baking soda. For a darker shade, they used copper filings, or even leeches mixed with wine and vinegar.

Hairstyles in ancient Rome changed over time. Pictured here is a bust of a Roman woman from around 160–170 CE.

Ancient Chinese pottery shows different updo hairstyles that women wore at the time.

In ancient Asia, the Chinese stained their nails with egg whites, vegetable dyes, and beeswax. Long painted nails were a symbol of wealth. So the wealthy wore gold and silver colors, and they wore bejeweled nail guards to protect their nails. Unmarried Chinese girls wore their hair long and braided. Married women combed their hair back and wound it into knots. Medieval Japanese women wore their hair long and loose. As time passed, styles changed. Women began sweeping their hair into updos and decorating them with pins and jeweled combs.

Styles by Culture

Throughout history, hairstyles from countries in Africa varied by groups of people. The Maasai warriors from eastern Africa tied their front hair into sections of tiny braids. The rest of their hair flowed loose down to their waists. Non-warriors and women often shaved their heads to beat the heat.

In central Africa, the Mangbetu women wore many thin braids. They arranged the plaits into a basket shape at the tops of their heads. Sometimes small animal bones decorated this common hairstyle. Other women chose to cover their long ponytails with headscarves and leaves.

A woman at the Maasai Mara National Reserve in Kenya keeps her hair short.

Indigenous hairstyles varied from culture to culture in North America. Creek and Chickasaw women wore their hair in buns or topknots. Navajo and Pueblo women often wore their hair in a twist at the back of their head. It was known as the chongo.

Lakota and Blackfeet men cut their hair to show grief or shame. Lenape and Iroquois warriors shaved the sides of their heads but left hair running down the middle. This was known as a roach, Mohawk, or Mohican hairstyle.

Thayendanegea, also known as Joseph Brant, was a Mohawk leader during the American Revolution who wore the Mohawk hairstyle.

Chapter 2

TRENDSETTING STYLES

We can find the latest hair and nail trends online and in magazines. Social media influencers rock hair and nail styles that get millions of likes and heart emoji.

The biggest stars shine bright with supercool hair colors. Members of the Korean boy band BTS are often seen with their hair dyed in bright pastel and metallic colors. Blackpink's Lisa Manoban, rapper Dawn, and singer Amber Liu are known for their rainbow hair colors.

Other stars such as singer Ariana Grande make their hairstyle their signature. Grande is known for her spunky high ponytail. But she loves to mix it up it too.

Celebrities and social media influencers keep their nails in the spotlight too. Icons such as Kylie Jenner and Selena Gomez often wear long, coffin-shaped nails in tie-dyed colors, plaids, and prints to match their moods.

THE SEVEN MEMBERS OF BTS ATTEND THE 2017 AMERICAN MUSIC AWARDS.

Style Icon

Ariana Grande loves a sky-high ponytail, and she knows how to make each one special. She

uses hair jewelry, extensions, crimpers, bangs, and other fun accessories. She also adds different colors to change her look. When she does wear her hair down, she usually straightens her natural curls.

Grande rocks her signature ponytail in 2016.

13

In 2019, Gomez decorated her nails in real crystals to walk the red carpet at the American Music Awards. Jenner has an Instagram page dedicated to her nail looks. The page shows off her multicolored nails to millions of followers.

Jenner shows off her detailed nail designs.

Red Carpet Looks

Child star Marsai Martin switches up her hairstyle for each red-carpet event. The fifteen-year-old showed up to an event in 2019 wearing a sleek braided bun dressed up with super-trendy-styled baby hairs along her hairline. That same year, she wore her natural hair in a free-flowing Afro on *Good Morning America*.

Marsai poses for a photo at the Chrysalis Butterfly Ball in 2019.

Sometimes Marsai adds extensions for a fuller, longer look. One such style was the long ponytail she wore at *The Lion King* movie premiere. When Marsai wears box braids, she lets them hang down her back or sweeps them up in a high side pony. Marsai dresses up her looks with hairpins and stylish beads.

Marsai styles her hair for red-carpet events, including the 2019 premiere of *The Lion King*.

That's a Fact!

American ballroom dancer Irene Castle helped to popularize the bob hairstyle in the early twentieth century. She cut her hair short around 1915. Many women liked the look and decided to try it. Short hair is harder to keep in place, so the bobby pin was invented.

Irene Castle

Chapter 3

TOOLS, TIPS, AND TRICKS

Creating your own styles is easy and fun. Look around your home for a few simple hair and nail tools.

To achieve Grande's high ponytail, you need strong elastic bands to keep your hair sky-high. A good hair pomade will keep your baby hairs in place.

Different types of hairbrushes can help to style hair in new and creative ways.

For many of Marsai's looks, you will need a light hair pomade to moisturize your scalp and a rattail comb to get precise parts. You'll also need strong fingers to braid sections of hair into tight rows.

If you're craving a new hair color, ask your hairstylist or an adult for help. And be careful! Adding color to your hair can leave it brittle and dry if you aren't taking proper care of it. Some hairstyles require heated hair tools such as curling irons, straighteners, and blow-dryers. When using hot tools, make sure you have adult supervision.

ADDING BRIGHT COLORS TO HAIR CAN BE FUN, BUT MAKE SURE TO HAVE AN ADULT HELP YOU.

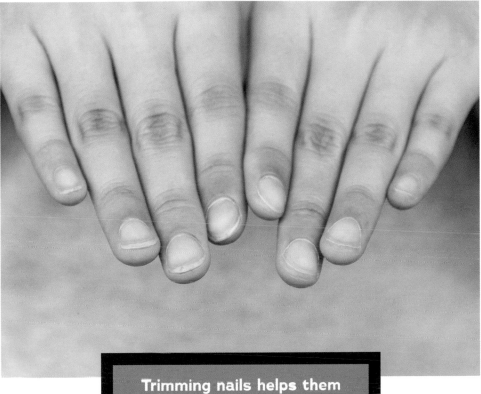

Trimming nails helps them stay healthy and keeps them at the length you want.

At-Home Manicure

To polish your look, try these steps for a perfect manicure at home. First, gently remove any old polish with nail polish remover. Then use a nail clipper to trim your nails to the length you want. You can use a nail file to shape your nails. Some people like their nail tips square. Some prefer a more rounded look.

Then apply a clear base coat to help your polish last longer. Finally, design the colorful look of your dreams. Using your favorite colors from your collection, apply two thin coats of nail polish. If it's hard to polish your writing hand, ask a family member or friend for help. Let each coat of polish dry for at least five minutes, and you're done.

Painting nails is a great way to spend time with friends.

Chapter 4

HAIR AND NAIL CARE

Healthy hair and nails start on the inside. Vitamin A in foods like carrots and sweet potatoes help keep your scalp and hair moisturized. Foods like eggs are full of vitamin B, which boosts hair and nail growth. Vitamin C, found in citrus fruits, bell peppers, and green vegetables, helps strengthen nails. The nutrients in dark green, leafy vegetables will make your hair soft and vibrant.

It's important to eat healthful foods so your body gets the vitamins and nutrients it needs.

Eating three balanced meals a day is great for your hair and nails. Small snacks can help too. Walnuts can protect your hair against sun damage. Blueberries may help prevent breakage.

That's a Fact!

You can donate your hair to people experiencing hair loss. Before the big chop, get a parent's or guardian's permission to donate. Charities such as Hair We Share or Wigs for Kids require at least 8 inches (20 cm) of hair. Some groups don't accept hair that has been colored, bleached, or dreadlocked. Hair donations help kids and adults who are experiencing hair loss to feel more self-confident.

Healthy Hair and Nail Habits

Keeping your hair clean and conditioned helps it stay healthy. Regular trims get rid of frayed ends and can boost hair growth. Using hair oils, if you have a dry scalp, and protecting your hair at night with a satin scarf can keep it from drying out and breaking off while you

TRIMMING OR CUTTING YOUR HAIR HELPS GET RID OF DAMAGED ENDS. ASK AN ADULT FOR HELP.

sleep. Managing your stress can also help prevent hair breakage. So remember to practice excellent self-care.

Having healthy nails requires proper care and hygiene. Wash your hands often. Try to avoid biting your nails. This introduces bacteria and fungi, which can damage your nails. Applying a clear coat can help protect your

Washing hands helps prevent the spread of germs and bacteria.

Lotions or hand creams help keep skin soft.

nails and prevent breakage. But remember that your nails need a chance to breathe. Having nail polish on all the time can weaken your nails.

With these tips and tricks, you're well on your way to healthy, stylish hair and nails!

Fashion Hack

Some nail designs seem tricky. But you can create your own fun nail art at home! Can you find a loofah no one is using? It can make a cool scale pattern. Once your base color polish is dry, place the loofah's netting over your nail and paint over it with another color. It creates an instant design.

Are you a polka-dot fan? Choose two colors you like. Use one to paint your nails. Then dip the tip of a bobby pin into the second color. Use the bobby pin to dot your nails. Voila—you have fabulous nail art.

Glossary

baby hair: small, fine, wispy hairs around the edges of the hairline

box braid: a three-strand braid or plait that is divided into a square-shaped section

brittle: easily broken

extension: an artificial hairpiece that can be attached to someone's hair to add fullness or length

henna: a plant-based dye used to decorate or color hair and skin

influencer: someone who makes money by sharing opinions on social media

plait: three or more pieces of hair woven into a braid

pomade: a hairstyling product used to change the texture or shape of hair, or to hold a hairstyle in place

ponytail: a hairstyle that has all the hair tied up at the back with the ends hanging free

trend: the latest style

Learn More

Anton, Carrie. *The Skin & Nails Book: Care & Keeping Advice for Girls.* Middleton, WI: American Girl, 2018.

Hair Facts for Kids
https://kids.kiddle.co/Hair

KidsHealth: Your Nails
https://kidshealth.org/en/kids/your-nails.html

Martin, Mari, and John Willis. *The Amazing Hairstyles Book.* New York: AV2 by Weigl, 2017.

Science Kids: Hair Facts
http://www.sciencekids.co.nz/sciencefacts/humanbody/hair.html

Wilson, Lakita. *My Amazing Makeup.* Minneapolis: Lerner Publications, 2022.

Index

Photo Acknowledgments

Image credits: Christine Osborne Pictures/Alamy Stock Photo, p. 5; lm_rohitbhakar/ Shutterstock.com, p. 6; Lanmas/Alamy Stock Photo, p. 7; Shan_shan/Shutterstock.com, p. 8; Nikolay Antonov/Shutterstock.com, p. 9; Classic Image/Alamy Stock Photo, p. 10; Featureflash Photo Agency/Shutterstock.com, p. 12; Tinseltown/Shutterstock.com, p. 13; Larry Busacca/ Getty Images for Aquafina FlavorSplash, p. 14; Kathy Hutchins/Shutterstock.com, p. 15; Jeffrey Mayer/Alamy Stock Photo, p. 16; Lebrecht Music & Arts/Alamy Stock Photo, p. 17; New Africa/ Shutterstock.com, p. 19; Gorlov-KV/Shutterstock.com, p. 20; BK_graphic/Shutterstock.com, p. 21; Maskot/agency/Getty Images, p. 22; Svetlana Lukienko/Shutterstock.com, p. 24; David Prado Perucha/Shutterstock.com, p. 25; Joshua Resnick/Shutterstock.com, p. 26; ANURAK PONGPATIMET/Shutterstock.com, p. 27; Prostock-studio/Shutterstock.com, p. 28.

Cover: id-art/Shutterstock.com; sklyareek/Shutterstock.com; Iakov Filimonov/Shutterstock .com.